What are...

LAKES

Andy Owen
and
Miranda Ashwell

Heinemann
LIBRARY

First published in Great Britain by Heinemann Library
Halley Court, Jordan Hill, Oxford OX2 8EJ
a division of Reed Educational and Professional Publishing Ltd.
Heinemann is a registered trademark of Reed Educational and Professional Publishing Ltd.

OXFORD FLORENCE PRAGUE MADRID ATHENS
MELBOURNE AUCKLAND KUALA LUMPUR SINGAPORE TOKYO
IBADAN NAIROBI KAMPALA JOHANNESBURG GABORONE
PORTSMOUTH NH (USA) CHICAGO MEXICO CITY SAO PAULO

Designed by Susan Clarke
Illustrations by Oxford Illustrators (maps pp.23, 25, 27), Hardlines (pp.14 & 15) and Nicki Wise (p.18)
Printed in Hong Kong

03 02 01 00 99
10 9 8 7 6 5 4 3 2 1

ISBN 0 431 02367 0

British Library Cataloguing in Publication Data

Owen, Andy
What are lakes?. – (Heinemann first library)
1. Lakes – Juvenile literature
I. Title II. Ashwell, Miranda III. Lakes
551.4'82

This book is also available in hardback (ISBN 0 431 02360 3)

Acknowledgements
The Publishers would like to thank the following for permission to reproduce photographs: Aerofilms, p.5; Barnaby's Picture Library/Carlos Hall Elmer, p.17; Bruce Coleman Ltd/Dieter & Mary Plage, p.16; FLPA/David Hosking, p.20; Geo Aerial, p.6; NRSC, pp.22, 24, 26; Oxford Scientific Films/ Tony Bomford & Tim Borrill, p.7; Planet Earth, p.11 (Sean Avery), p.4 (Ivor Edmonds); Robert Harding Picture Library/Paolo Koch, p.28; Science Photo Library/Worldsat International Inc, pp.12, 29; South Australian Tourism Commission p.10; Still Pictures, p.19 (Nigel Dickinson), p.9 (Mark Edwards), p.21 (Bittu Sahgal), p.8 (Jorgen Schytte); Zefa/Breig, p.13.

Cover photograph: Planet Earth / Ivor Edwards

Our thanks to Betty Root for her comments in the preparation of this book.

Contents

Some words are shown in bold, **like this**. You can find out what they mean by looking in the Glossary.

How lakes are made

Water collects in dips in the land to make a lake. This lake was made by water **flowing** from the melting ice.

A lake made by melting ice

A deep lake in England

Ice cut this deep **valley** thousands of years ago. Water has collected at the bottom of the valley to make a lake.

Lakes and rivers

Water **flows** in and out of lakes. A small river brings **fresh water** into this lake. On the other side of the lake, the water flows into a river.

The river at the bottom of the photo flows out of the lake

Rivers carry sand and mud into the lake. This is dropped in **layers**. One day all the lake will be filled with sand and mud.

This river drops its mud as it meets the lake

Drying out

This small lake in Africa was filled with water during heavy rain storms. It only took a few days of rain to fill the lake.

Animals and people need water to drink

Without rain, lakes become dry. In hot weather this happens very quickly. These people dug a hole to find water deep in the ground.

These girls must carry the water to their home

Salt water lakes

Most lakes have **fresh water**. In hot places some lakes are salty. These lakes are often very shallow and dry up easily.

Lake Eyre in Australia is a salty lake

When the lake dries up the salt is left behind on the soil. Plants cannot grow in the salty soil.

Salt was left behind when this lake dried up

The Great Lakes

A photo of the Great Lakes from space

There are five Great Lakes in North America.
The lakes are joined together by rivers.
People can travel from lake to lake.

People live in large cities beside the Great Lakes. Iron and coal are carried by boat to large factories in the cities.

A ship sailing out of a large city

Dams

A river valley before a lake is made

People make lakes. This **valley** is a good place to make a lake. The steep sides of these hills will hold the water.

People build a wall called a **dam** across rivers. The dam stops the river water **flowing** away.

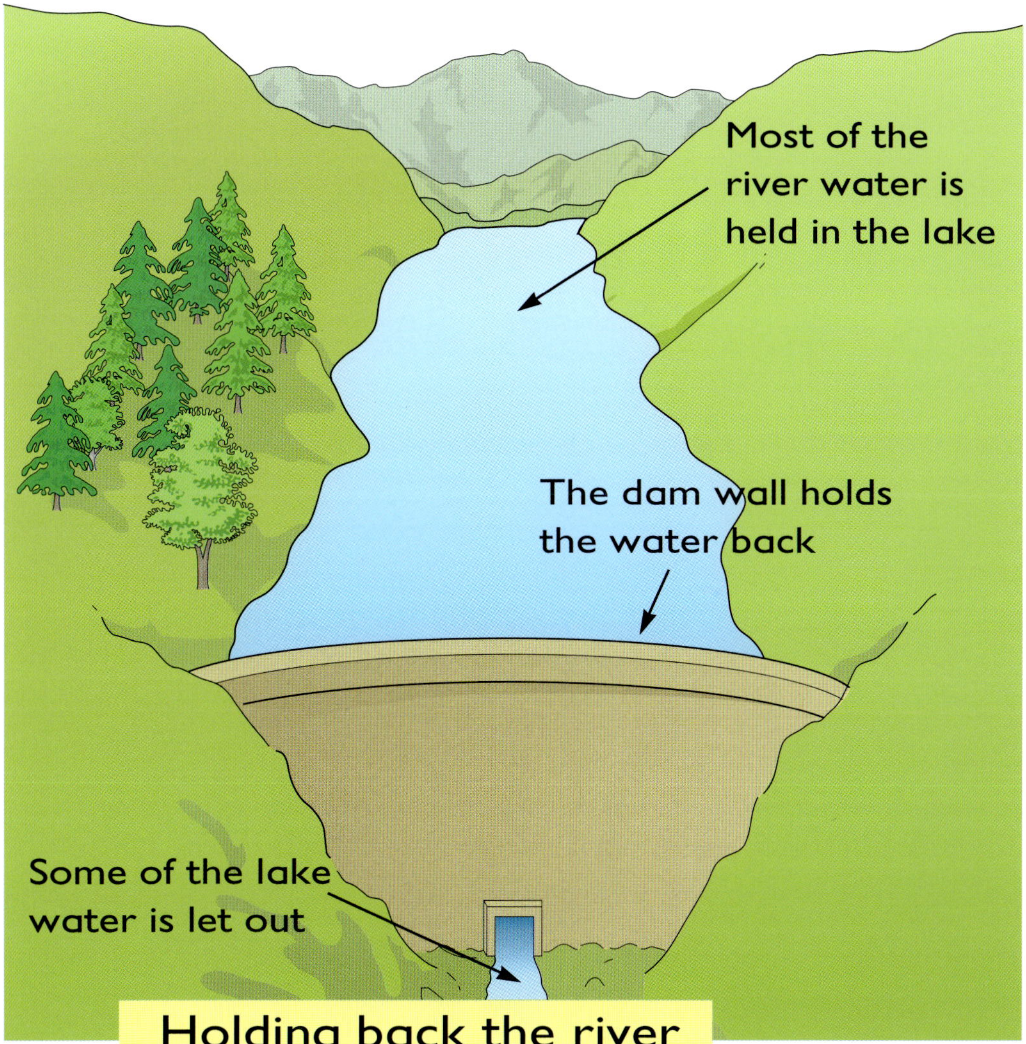

Holding back the river

Moving the water

This huge **dam** is on the Colorado River in America. This dam was built so people living in the desert could have water.

The Glen Canyon Dam

Water has to be moved from the lake to where people live. People made a **channel** that takes the water across the desert to the city.

This channel carries water from the lake to the city

Using water

We use water in many ways. We need water for cleaning, drinking and washing. You use more than 500 glasses of water every day.

How we use water

This lake is drying out because so much water has been used. Lots of rain is needed to fill this lake.

All this dried mud used to be covered by water

Large and small lakes

Everyone in a village is helping to build a small dam

These people in India are making their own **dam** from mud and rocks. Now they will be able to grow food when there is no rain.

This dam is being made from steel and concrete

This large dam is also in India. The water will be used by thousands of people. The dam costs a lot of money to build.

Lake map 1

This photo was taken from an aeroplane. You can see a small lake. A small river **flows** into the lake at the top of the photo.

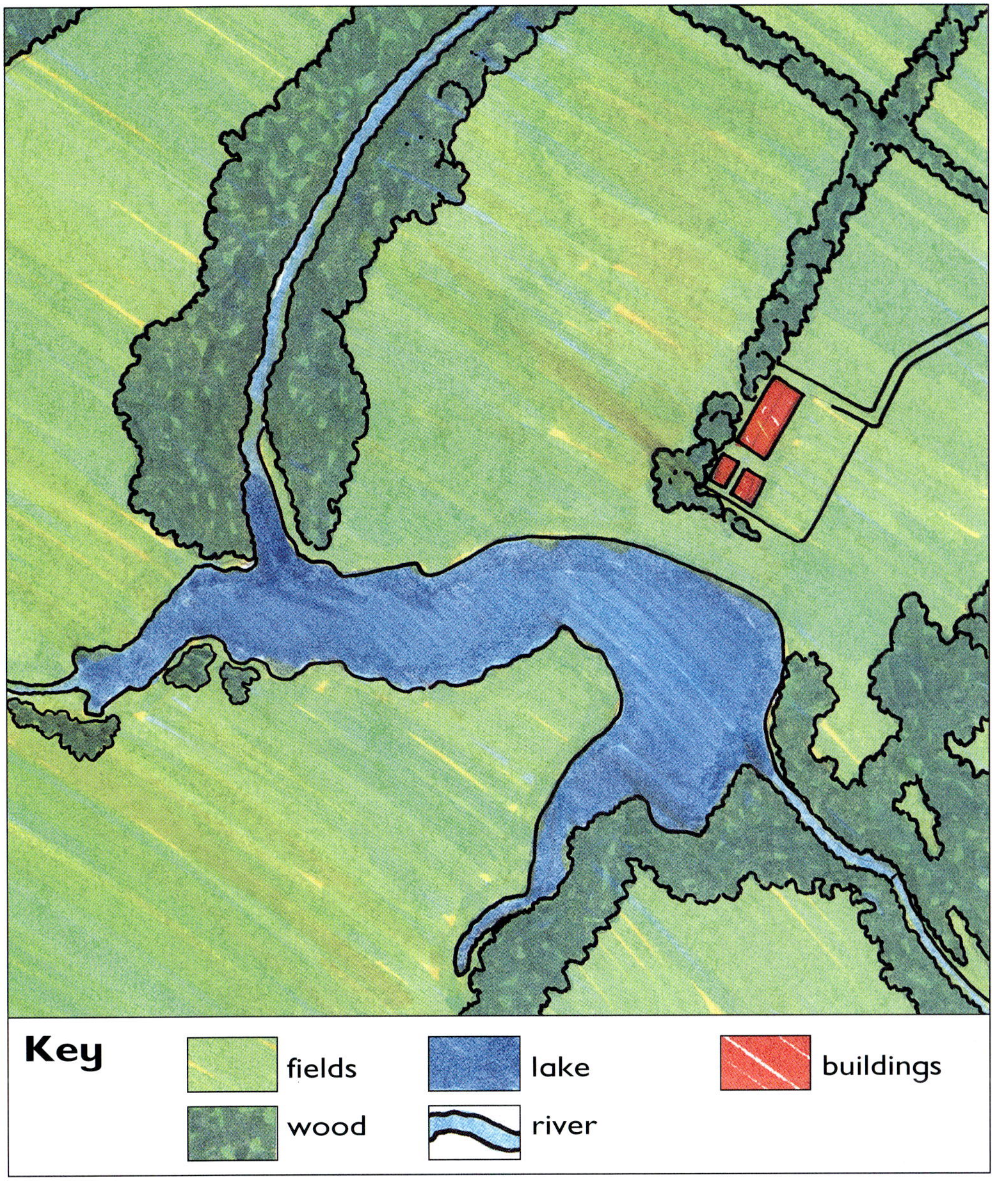

Maps are pictures of the land. This map shows us the same place as the photo. The key tells us what each colour means.

Lake map 2

This photo is of the same lake. The lake looks smaller but you can see more of the land around it.

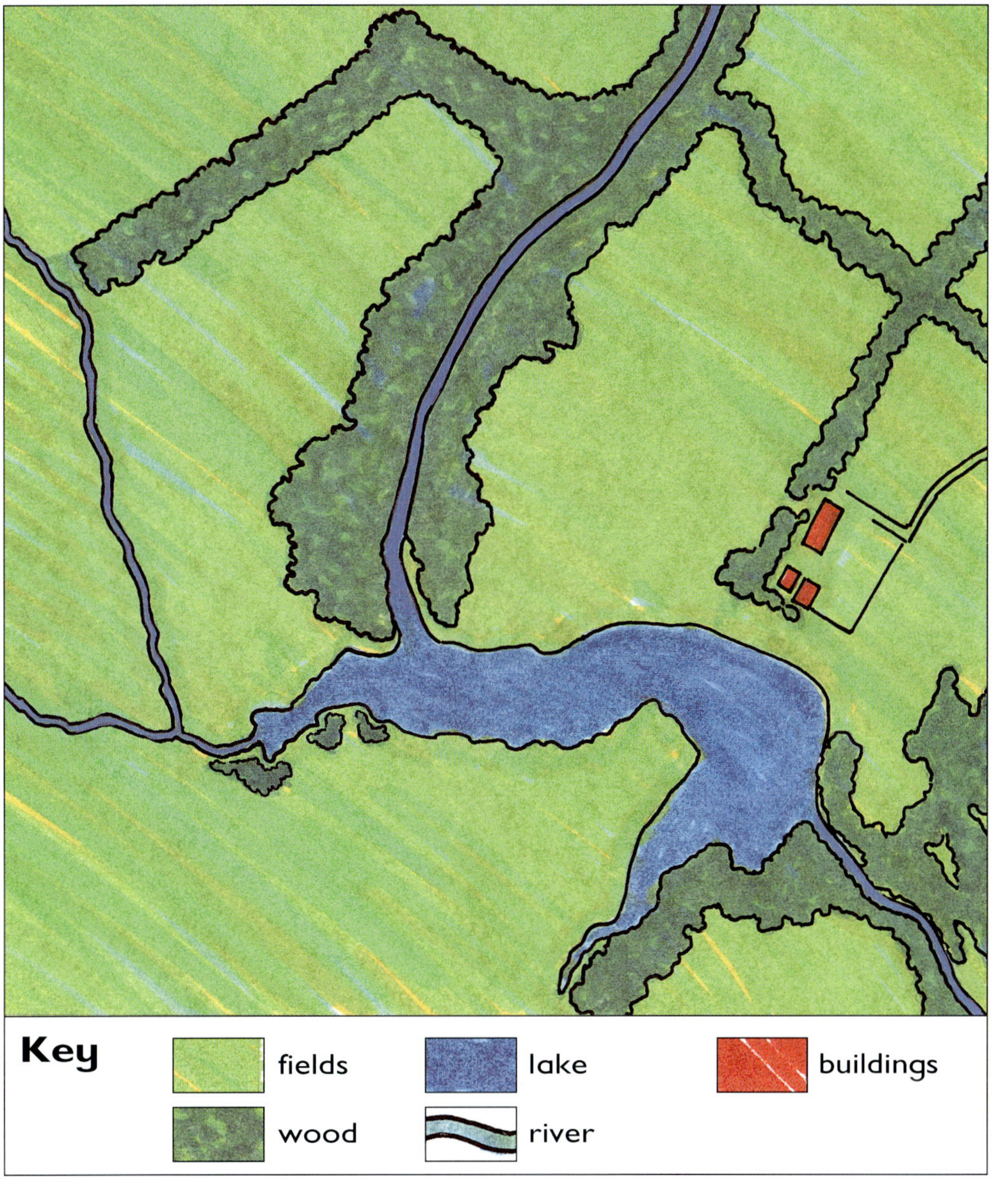

The thin blue lines show rivers. Some of these rivers are difficult to see in the photo because they are hidden by trees.

Lake map 3

In this photo the lake looks even smaller. We can also see part of a larger lake. This lake has a **dam** wall.

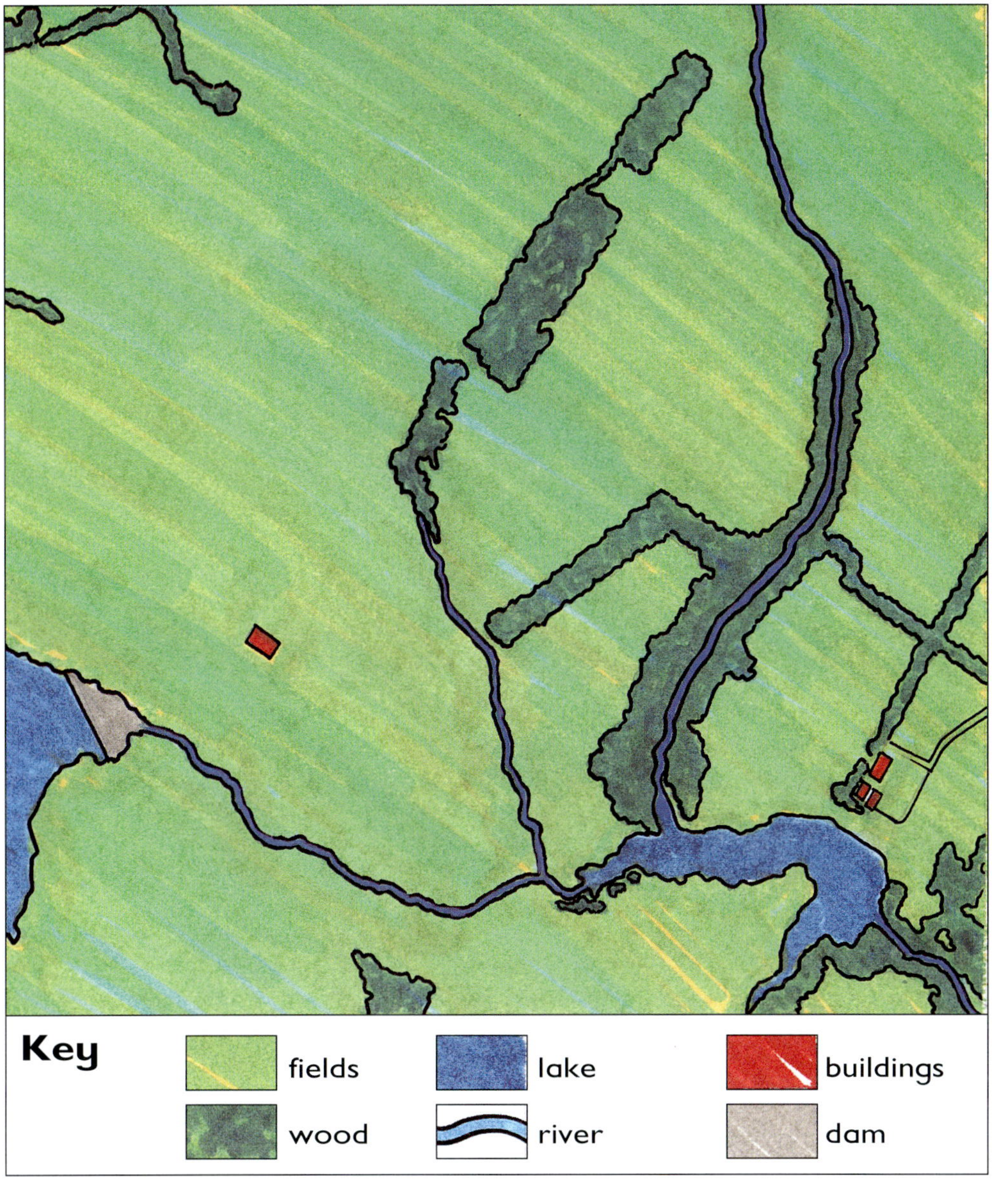

This map makes it easy to see that a river joins the two lakes. The river **flows** through the dam and into the smaller lake.

Amazing lake facts

Lake Baikal in Russia has more water in it than any other lake in the world. It is 1,900 metres deep so it is the deepest lake in the world.

The Great Lakes in the USA are the largest group of lakes in the world. It is 1,800 kilometres from one end of the Great Lakes to the other end.

Glossary

channel this is the path a river takes. Some channels are made by people

dam wall built across a river to hold back the water

flowing movement of water

fresh water water that is not salty

layers thicknesses or levels

valley low land between hills. Rivers often flow along a valley

More books to read

Helena Ramsey. *Step-by-step: Rivers and Lakes.* Franklin Watts, 1996

You may need help to read these books on lakes.

Nicola Barber. *Rivers, Ponds and Lakes.* Evans Brothers, 1993

David Cummings. *Habitats: Rivers and Lakes.* Wayland, 1996

Neil Morris. *World's Top Ten Lakes.* Belitha Press, 1997

Index